Kelvin MacKenzie is th of all time, with a unic pages. He edited Brit *Sun* from 1981 to 1 with outrageous and front pages, GOTCHA; UP YOURS, DELORS and FREDDIE MY HAMSTER were recently in the top ten newspaper pages of all time in a television poll. After leaving *The Sun*, Kelvin joined Sky TV before becoming Chief Executive of The Wireless Group plc, which owned the national radio station TalkSport and several local stations. After the Wireless Group was bought by Ulster TV, Kelvin left to mastermind various business ventures and has returned to his old stomping ground, *The Sun*, as a star columnist.

THE
JOHN
PRESCOTT
KAMA
SUTRA

A modern interpretation of the
ancient guide to lovemaking, from the
Office of the Deputy Prime Minister

KELVIN MACKENZIE

JOHN BLAKE

Published by John Blake Publishing Ltd,
3 Bramber Court, 2 Bramber Road,
London W14 9PB, England

www.blake.co.uk

First published in hardback in 2006

ISBN 13: 978-1-84454-336-6
ISBN 10: 1-84454-336-6

British Library Cataloguing-in-Publication Data:

A catalogue record for this book is available from the British Library.

Design by www.envydesign.co.uk

Printed in Great Britain by Bookmarque

1 3 5 7 9 10 8 6 4 2

Papers used by John Blake Publishing are natural, recyclable
products made from wood grown in sustainable forests.
The manufacturing processes conform to the environmental
regulations of the country of origin.

JOHN Leslie Prescott, Labour MP and Deputy Prime Minister, is one of Britain's most controversial and frequently lampooned public figures. The Member for Hull East was most famous for his speeches of pure gibberish in the Commons, for punching an egg-thrower on the election trail and for riding around in TWO chauffeur-driven Jags. That was until his notorious affair with his diary secretary, Tracey Temple. This light-hearted spoof rewrites the *Kama Sutra* for the great man, with each sexual scenario given a verdict by Prescott, every single word of which has been made up. Although our positions are feats of imagination based on actual episodes in Prescott's life, there is no suggestion he is partial to any of them.

CONTENTS

PART ONE
THE JOHN PRESCOTT KAMA SUTRA 1

PART TWO
JOHN PRESCOTT – A SERIES OF UNFORTUNATE EVENTS 93

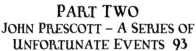

PART THREE
GIT OF THE GAB – PRESCOTT'S TEN FAVOURITE CHAT-UP LINES 115

PART FOUR
THE BUTT STOPS HERE
TEN PRESCOTT JOKES 119

PART FIVE
HE'S HISTORY – PREZZA AS TEN GREAT
SHAGGERS OF THE PAST 129

PART SIX
ASK UNCLE PREZZA 141

PART SEVEN
COMMONS AS MUCK – TEN MPS
WHO CAME BEFORE HIM 165

PART EIGHT
GRUBBY'S UP – PRESCOTT'S
RECIPE FOR LOVE 179

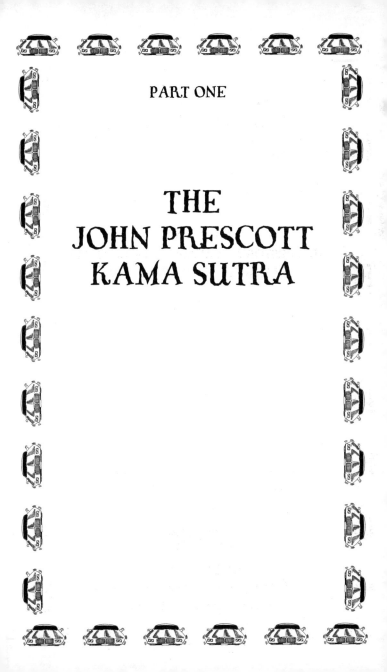

PART ONE

THE
JOHN PRESCOTT
KAMA SUTRA

CHAPTER ONE

SEDUCTION

Lovemaking is not something to be rushed into. Quality sex is worth waiting for. A couple must share love and respect and know each other well, physically and spiritually, before they can make full sex work well for them both. When it comes to foreplay, Prescott recommends a combination of subtlety and sensuousness. Here are a selection of his seductive ploys.

HOSTESS WITH THE MOSTEST

A very specialised and subtle mode of seduction normally employed by the DPM on an aircraft, from which the woman – in this instance a stewardess – has no chance of escape.

HOW TO DO IT: Timing is everything. The stewardess must be about to serve the male passenger fruit. As she offers a pear, the man must stare into her chest and remark with a lecherous grin, 'Nice pear.' This gambit lives or dies on the choice of fruit available; 'nice apples' or 'nice bananas' are unlikely to convey the intended meaning. Should the hostess be serving melons, however, it is your lucky day. Since further intimacy on an aircraft is hard to organise, especially with a uniformed member of staff, the object of this exercise is primarily the schoolboy thrill of getting away with a sexist remark to which she is powerless to object. In extraordinarily rare cases involving women who are intellectually challenged, it might lead to the disclosure of her phone number.

PREZZA SAYS: *Ayup. I remember first time I flew ter New York. Beforehand, I rang British Airways 'n said, "Ow long is flight from London to New York?" The bird says, 'Um, just a minute, sir.' 'Bloody 'ell,' I thought to meself, 'that's quick.' It were never only a chuffin' minute really, though.*

THE HAND UP THE SKIRT

An introductory gambit much favoured by Prescott as the essential preliminary to a night of romance. First attempted within seconds of meeting another MP's wife back in 1978, Prescott still maintains this artful move as a key weapon in his sexual armoury – using it to winning effect with his most recent lover Tracey Temple.

HOW TO DO IT: The man uses one hand to force his intended partner up against a hard surface (a wall or door, for instance). Taking advantage of the few seconds during which she is too shocked to speak, he places his other hand – as the position's name describes – simply 'up the skirt'. A discerning woman may react to this with a scream or a slap, at which point the rebuffed male may simply shrug his shoulders and move on. Needier women may be flattered by the attention and proceed to the next stage.

PREZZA SAYS: *There's nowt better than grabbin' a lass and coppin' a feel of her undercarriage. But I always resist shoving both hands up her skirt – like me granddad always said, 'A bird in't hand is worth two in 'er bush.'*

GOING-DOWN

A moment of opportunist magic during which the DPM takes advantage of the privacy and inescapability of an enclosed space to derive a brief thrill from fondling a woman's breasts or buttocks. Subordinates are always flattered by the sexual attentions of powerful men, so this move rarely fails to lead to greater intimacy ... especially with diary secretaries.

HOW TO DO IT: The man engineers a situation where he is alone with his intended partner in a lift. He hits the button for the floor furthest from where they are — thus maximising the time available. He sidles up to the woman (best done from behind to limit her reaction time) and places his hands lasciviously on the intimate area of his choice.

To increase the window of opportunity in a lift situation, the man simply needs to jump up and down a few times, thus activating the safety cut-out mechanism which will bring the lift swiftly to a halt. During the panic that ensues, the man may 'fall' inadvertently against the woman, and continue with the Hand Up The Skirt manoeuvre or, if he's really lucky, she may fall into his arms anyway, and be willing to have her mind taken off the imminent danger by full-scale lovemaking until rescued by the emergency services.

PREZZA SAYS: *Eeeh, I love lifts, me. I were once in a lift with a stunnin' lass, when she suddenly strips off her blouse 'n bra, chucks 'em on t'floor and says, 'Ayup! Make uz feel like a woman.' So I unbuttoned me own shirt, threw it on t'floor and said, 'Here, woman... iron that!'*

CHAPTER TWO

FOREPLAY

Assuming that any of Prescott's three basic seduction techniques were successful (and let's face it, how can they fail?), we are ready to move on to the next stage.

UP TO HIS NECK IN SLEAZE

Oh, how Prescott enjoyed twisting the knife in John Major's mortally wounded Government in 1996. 'The Tories are up to their necks in sleaze,' he announced melodramatically, to rapturous applause. And now, joy of joys, he is hoist by his own petard. He has reaped what he has sown and his chickens have come home to roost. Here's a little warm-up position that might remind the heavyweight hypocrite of the words that came back to haunt him.

HOW TO DO IT: Essentially, the man places his head between the ample breasts of his partner until he is visible only from the neck down. In keeping with tradition, he must then shake his head from side to side uttering the words, 'Flubble, blubble, blubble.'

PREZZA SAYS: *It weren't my fault I got mixed up with Tracey Temple. It were 18 years o' chuffin' Tories. No offence, Trace, but, if Thatcher hadn't done away with free eye tests, I probably would never 'av touched yer with me barge pole.*

BUST ROUTE

Prescott likes few things better than opening something – pay cheques, for instance; the door to a chauffered limo; or the absurd bus lane he opened

on the M4's busiest stretch, causing instant jams. Here's a naughty game inspired by the DPM's love of the grand opening.

HOW TO DO IT: The woman is naked but wrapped in a pink ribbon covering her most intimate areas. The man is suited and booted, and armed with a pair of scissors. But worry not – this is not a scene from a slasher movie! Instead, the man gently approaches his partner and, turning his head with a cheesy grin for make-believe cameras, snips away at the ribbon. As it falls to the ground, he announces, 'I declare this bust route open for business!'

PREZZA SAYS: *I used to love going on t'bus, me. That was before I got me two Jags, mind. I remember once I were sitting on the number 42 in Hull, when this old feller got on and stood next to me. 'E 'ad this old walking stick that kept slippin' when the bus moved, so I said, 'You wanna get a bit of rubber on the end of yer stick, mate.' He looked at me right narked and said, 'If yer dad had put a bit o' rubber on the end o' his stick, I'd have a seat by now.' Chuffin' Tory.*

COOKING-THE CHIPOLATA

An intimate and fun roleplaying preamble to sex, inspired by Tracey Temple's description of the DPM's tiny appendage.

HOW TO DO IT: The man, standing naked, indicates that owing to his expanding waistline he has not seen his honourable member in years – and challenges his partner to find it. She, naked but for a Deerstalker hat and the magnifying glass she is clutching, gives him a full examination but finds nothing. A second sweep turns up an appendage which might be classed as the male organ and, in the absence of anything else, has to do. The female, using any means at her disposal, sets about trying to arouse the tiny todger and must stifle her laughter when she discovers it is already fully engorged.

PREZZA SAYS: By 'eck, that Tracey Temple said I only had a chipolata. Lying cow. And then it were all over the Tory press! I should 'av known she weren't impressed, mind – the first time we 'ad sex, she says to me, 'OK, Jumbo, I'm ready… you can take your little finger out now…' But I'd already completed me dispatch box, as it 'appens! Dozy mare!

CRUEL BRITANNIA

Another kinky number, inspired by the infamous dousing of our portly hero in ice water at the Brits. There was the tubby idler, well into his 50s,

pathetically trying to hype New Labour's 'Cool Britannia' credentials by rubbing shoulders with pop stars when suddenly Danbert Nobacon, a man Prescott had never heard of before that moment, emptied a bucket over him. Prescott went from Cool Britannia to Raging Britannia in a nanosecond.

HOW TO DO IT: In this imaginative scenario, the man's sexual urges are repeatedly brought to a crescendo, then instantly defused, until he can bear no more. Preparation is crucial – the woman must have at her disposal several buckets of iced water. Each time, she teases her man into a state of arousal by fawning over him and making him feel wanted and acceptable (giving him a home-made ID pass marked 'VIP' will help). Suddenly, and without warning, she must drench him. For his part, he must stomp around swearing, puce with rage, before settling back for the teasing cycle to begin again.

PREZZA SAYS: *Blimey, I remember them Brits well. The wife was worried about me going, 'cos she'd heard about all the boozin' and bad behaviour. But I told 'er, 'I don't care what you've heard about me, I'm going.'*

TANTRIC PHONE SEX

Phone sex is a common enough diversion for lovers the world over. However, this Tantric version used with Tracey Temple can take many, many hours due to the DPM's inability ever to utter a coherent sentence.

HOW TO DO IT: The man and woman, both naked at their respective homes, must speak by telephone for hours in hushed tones. Crucially, they must never get to the point. If sexual gratification is achieved, the idea has failed. It is permissible, and understandable, for the woman to sleep through large parts of the conversation. To achieve true Tantric Phone Sex, the man must study and rehearse Prescott monologues.

A useful starting point would be Prezza's speech on urban regeneration, which is printed here verbatim (albeit translated into English), which will keep any potential partner on a slow simmer for hours: 'Coming from low demand, houses available, prices falling… Depends from area to area, but, if you go to the South, it's exactly the opposite. The choice is not normally between the North and South. It might be between Britain and Europe. You go down some street – no doubt it's there, and we have to do something about it, and our programmes are designed to do that – but if that's a picture of Newcastle, it's not the one I recognise and I bet none in the North-East do either.'

PREZZA SAYS: *Oooh, I love a bit o' dirty talk, me. But I've never understood this – when a bloke talks dirty to a woman, it's sexual harassment and he gets done fer it. When she talks dirty to 'im, it costs 'im £1.50 a chuffin' minute. That's 18 years of bloody Thatcher for you.*

GLOBES ALL WARMING

Prescott is fanatical about climate change. Playing the statesman on a recent trip abroad, he announced, 'Climate change is the biggest challenge facing the planet today.' Which is why he likes to take a 15 miles-per-gallon Jaguar on trips short enough for a baby to crawl. This scenario

adds a few degrees to the Earth's temperature…
and Prescott's lover.

HOW TO DO IT: Light a bonfire in the garden. Start
the car and leave it idling. Go indoors. Turn on every
appliance and every light. Put the heating on full. All
of this burns more energy and expels more
emissions. Now you're living Prescott-style. It's time
to turn your attention to HER. Wearing furry gloves
made from an endangered animal, rub your hands all
over her most curvaceous areas. Now her globes
are all warming! If she doesn't pass out from
heatstroke, sex may ensue.

PREZZA SAYS: *It's a right pain in the jacksy,
this global warmin'. No one really knows what's
goin' on. When I spoke at climate change
conference not so long back, I said to the
assembled experts that global warming was
happenin' a lot faster than I'd realised. Hundreds
of years to raise t'Earth's temperature a couple
of degrees? Bollocks! It had definitely got
warmer over the last couple of weeks. Then
someone pointed out to me that it was spring.
Well, make yer bloody minds up!*

THE BAWDROOM

There can surely be few grander settings in Britain for a furtive fumble than the Admiralty Boardroom. It was here that Admiral Lord Nelson hatched his battle plan for Trafalgar. Two hundred years later, it is here that weighty matters of State are still discussed by the most powerful people in the land. And it was here, in the Year of Our Lord 2003, that the Rt Hon John Prescott MP, Deputy Prime Minister of the United Kingdom and Northern Ireland, First Secretary of State, didst fondle the breasts of his diary secretary.

HOW TO DO IT: Sadly, access to the Admiralty Boardroom is strictly limited to Government Ministers, Navy chiefs, civil servants and others fleecing taxpayers of £600,000 a year. So the oak-panelled splendour may have to be bought from B&Q. Portraits of distinguished Navy figures will also need to be bought or, if there is time, painted.

Begin by admiring the portraits as though in awe, as though humbled by each character's influence on the history of our great nation. Your partner will do the same. Maintain a reverent, hushed tone. This is your moment. Emitting a

porcine grunt, shatter the serenity with a sudden lunge for her chest and an attempted snog. It cannot fail to melt her heart.

PREZZA SAYS: *They always say there's no such thing as a free lunge – but I'm livin' proof there is! It warms t'cockles of me working-class 'eart to cop a feel with them silly toffs in their daft 'ats lookin' down on uz. Specially that Nelson – he looks perfectly 'armless! Geddit? I tell yer, if I was made o' chocolate, I'd eat meself.*

CHAPTER THREE

SEXUAL POSITIONS

No matter how inept or cack-handed you might be in carrying out the previous manoeuvres, one thing's certain — if you've got a bit of dosh, two chauffeur-driven Jags, several well-stocked bolt-holes around the country and happen to have the ear of the Prime Minister, your partner will be gagging for it.

Now it's time to enter into full sexual congress, and bring her to heights of passion that have hitherto only occurred in her dreams. That's the plan, anyway. The following techniques will help to achieve this, and have become firm Prescott favourites. Possibly.

MEMORIAL SERVICING

The grieving process can be slow and painful. So why not lighten your mood with a burst of passionate oral sex, like Prescott and Tracey Temple after a poignant service at St Paul's Cathedral for British soldiers killed in Iraq?

HOW TO DO IT: This is non-stop roleplaying fun! Dress head to foot in black, because for a good hour or two you're going to be 'mourners'. Pop along to a funeral or memorial service. Anyone's will do! Mingle with distressed relatives, shake hands grimly, stare at the ground. Pose for photographers. You may be bursting with lust — but keep schtum. Do NOT burst into giggles!

Once the whole tedious business is over, tear back to his flat and rip off your funeral garb. It'll help if the woman has worn her very sexiest black lace undies to the service. After an hour or two of agonising frustration in church, the man will do ANYTHING to satisfy his woman.

PREZZA SAYS: *It's well known round our way – there's nothing quite like a stiff to raise a stiffy. Though I thought it were a bit much for Tracey to say she thought my John Thomas had already been cremated. She's got a mouth on 'er, that lass!*

SHAG-IN THE JAG

Nothing works better for an instant release of tension before a speech on, for example, climate change. The man and his lover are whisked along in the seductive comfort of leather upholstery as the gaz-guzzling limo pumps pollution gratifyingly into the atmosphere. One drawback to this position, however, is that it burns off calories – something Prescott loathes, doing anything he can to avoid walking even the shortest distance.

HOW TO DO IT:
Speed is of the essence. In full view of photographers, the man enters the

car fully suited – and must disembark fully suited less than 30 seconds later. It is therefore ESSENTIAL for both man and woman to partially disrobe the very moment the door closes. A short course of foreplay in the hotel or conference centre before departure is advisable – as are blacked-out windows in the Jag (standard Government issue).

PREZZA SAYS: *There's nowt that appeals more to me working-class roots than a quick leg-over in t'back o' chauffeur-driven Jag. Aside from owt else, it stops wife's 'air gettin blown about in t'wind... specially if she's not there!*

OPEN ALL HOURS

Danger could so easily be John Prescott's middle name – if he could spell it! This position is notable for the incredible element of risk – Prescott used to have sex with Tracey Temple standing up behind the open door to his private office as civil servants worked a few feet away.

HOW TO DO IT: For full effect, this is obviously best performed in an office. It can be done at home, but should then be performed behind the open front door, so there is some opportunity for the neighbours, the postman or the binman to catch you at it.

The man must attract his lover's attention by calling from the office, 'Take a letter, Ms Temple!' Within seconds of her sitting on the edge of his desk, she must be bundled behind the door where full coitus must take place, with requisite grunting, as embarrassed co-workers/passers-by within easy earshot put fingers in their ears, heads in their hands or ring the *Sun*.

PREZZA SAYS: *Oh yes, I like a bit of rumpy-pumpy stood up, but it's well 'ard to do. You have to take t'bird's full weight, so she needs to be light. In fact, that's main difference between a girlfriend and a missus – about three chuffin' stone!*

SHOW ME YOUR SPECIALS

A 'master and servant' roleplaying fantasy based on Prescott's early career as a waiter aboard Cunard cruise ships – a seething little class warrior ferrying bubbly to his superiors.

HOW TO DO IT: In this position, the man must fetch his partner anything she desires – and is finally rewarded with the most generous tip! Dress code: for him, the full waiter's uniform. For her: nothing. For two hours, he fetches food, drink and dessert to his naked companion on a silver salver, tugging his forelock and uttering obsequious remarks about her appearance and taste. At the end of the meal – horror of horrors – she cannot pay her bill. A Benny Hill-style chase ensues, after which she pays her 'waiter' in kind – and with interest!

PREZZA SAYS: I always wanted one of them posh birds when I were on t'cruise ships. I weren't much cop as a waiter, mind. Once, the chef had a go at me 'cos he found me starin' at a can of orange juice. It wasn't my fault, mind... it said 'concentrate' on the side. How were I supposed to know?

BOMBING FROM 15 FT

A dramatic but risky position for a man of Prescott's ample proportions and inspired by an infamous gaffe to a US senator in which the DPM asserted that British Harriers in action in the 'Balklands' and 'Kovosa' were bombing from just 15ft.

HOW TO DO IT: High ceilings are important – so, if possible, use one of the grand offices of Whitehall or, better still, a large and opulent grace-and-favour residence. Disrobe. Using a step-ladder, the man must scale a large wardrobe and crouch atop it as his lover waits expectantly on a bed beneath. Then, with a dramatic cry such as 'Geronimo' – or, in Prezza's case, 'Geromino' – he must dive on top of his partner, allowing her to take his colossal weight as he assumes the coital position of his choosing. Top bombing!

PREZZA SAYS: *The best thing about this one is t'exercise I get getting up the ladder. Doctor told us exercise is great for droppin' weight. Well, I took him at his word... I dropped me weight on Tracey whenever I got the chance!*

ADMIRALTY ARCH-BACK

A favourite position adopted at the £2.3 million grace-and-favour flat at Admiralty Arch where Prescott liked to service Tracey Temple. How he must have marvelled at the scene – before him, one of the finest views in London; beneath him, a youngish woman, not his wife; around him, an opulent 18th-century apartment for which he paid not a penny. For a working-class lad, it must have been tough to get over, but he just about managed it without too many crises of conscience.

HOW TO DO IT: Not easy. Procuring the sexual partner is straightforward enough. But try securing a dream flat and getting taxpayers to fund it without the long and tedious process of standing for Parliament. Nonetheless, a similar effect CAN be achieved by catching an open-top tourist bus around London, sitting on the upper deck and timing coitus for the moment it enters Trafalgar Square. If you have managed to get on the tour without buying a ticket, you're VERY close to that 'Prescott feeling'.

PREZZA SAYS: Now then, I love that flat. People often ask me 'ow I sleep at night. Well, I always sleep like a chuffin' baby there. And the dreams I 'ave, they blow me mind sometimes. Once, I dreamt I was the most handsome and powerful man in England, with unlimited transport, all the money I could ever want, a wife and a girlfriend, luxurious homes and people bowing to me every whim. And then I woke up... and realised I were an ugly gut-bucket. Who cares? The rest were true, though!

SITTING-PRETTY

Old age will not be hard on Prescott – he has a £1.5 million pension package to fall back on. Not for him the struggle facing millions of lesser mortals whose pensions are worth buttons… he'll be wallowing around on £60,000 a year, and he's already got his own croquet set to keep him busy in his old age.

HOW TO DO IT: Find an idyllic spot – a beach, perhaps. Or maybe a Government-owned country estate to which you have exclusive access. The man should settle himself down on a comfy pile of cash – then let his partner settle herself down on him. He can then relax and enjoy the moment as someone else does all the work (the Prescott career, in microcosm).

PREZZA SAYS: *Ah've got big plans for me retirement. Missus 'as already bought me a ten-piece jigsaw puzzle which looks right tricky. It says 2–3 years on t'box. I reckon it'll take me longer than that, mind.*

HORNY WOOD

In this oasis of tranquillity in rural Buckinghamshire, amid the silver birches, the herbaceous borders and the immaculate topiary, Prescott liked to relax by making languid love. Not to his wife, mind. No, the placidity of Dorneywood was generally shattered by the bestial grunts of Prescott and his lover. He adored this place. Its fig tree, its lily pond, its crunching gravel drive. Most of all he adored that it was all free – a gift from grateful taxpayers. What an aphrodisiac!

HOW TO DO IT: Clearly, this is a hard one to pull off, so to speak. Generally, you will need to ascend to high office to have any chance at all. Your best bet to simulate Prescott's passionate summer nights in the country is to take a tour round one of Britain's National Trust mansions, sneak off the beaten track and find a shady spot for a quick Deputy Prime Ministerial fumble.

PREZZA SAYS: *I were furious we 'ad ter give up Dorneywood – I loved it there. We 'ad a fire there once, ya know… int' library. It were terrible. Both me books got burned. Which were a shame – I hadn't finished colouring second one in.*

THE GRASPING DOG

Tracey Temple said she often dispensed sexual favours to Prescott as he struggled with ministerial papers. The struggle presumably being working out which way was up. This useful position leaves the man's hands free for any purpose – in Prescott's case, to count his enormous taxpayer-funded wages, to rifle documents relating to his gold-plated pension, or perhaps to sign orders building slum flats all over areas of natural beauty in the South-East.

HOW TO DO IT: In essence, without beating around the bush or putting too fine a point on it, this involves the man taking the woman while both are standing up. The man's weight is on his feet, leaving his arms free. Meanwhile, the woman, being bent double, exposes her back for the man to use as a makeshift 'desk' for his paperwork.

PREZZA SAYS: *When I'm in t'office, I like ter look busy, you know, making decisions about where taxpayers' money's being spent. It reminds people how important I am. Once, some bloke appeared in my office, so I showed him who was boss by picking up the phone and* pretending Tony Blair were on the other end. I said, 'Yeah, Tone, I've decided to give them £1.5 billion, and then when it's all done, if the Queen insists on the knighthood, I'll have to go along with it...' Then the bloke interrupted me by sayin', 'Sorry, Mr Prescott, there was a problem with the switchboard... I'm here to reconnect the phone lines...' The tosser made me look a right chump.

DEBT RELIEF

The thrill of living on the edge is encapsulated in this wonderful position inspired by Prescott's forgetful attitude to the law (as well as for marital fidelity). Prezza, it turned out, was presiding over colossal council tax rises for ordinary mortals while forgetting to pay his own. A charitable trust benevolently

coughed up for the Dorneywood council tax bill, while the big man paid a reduced rate for the Hull mansion. The taxpayer, presumably as unaware of their generosity as Prezza was, picked up the tab for the Admiralty Arch flat. But when this came to light Prezza stumped up the cash.

HOW TO DO IT: Forget to pay your council tax for months on end. Then, when the council sends officials round, have sex as they hammer on the door. This is living Prescott-style. Of course, since you are NOT John Prescott, you're likely to go to jail. But you'll be the toast of D-Wing once you've told them that for a few moments you lived like the great man.

PREZZA SAYS: *I did really forget to pay me tax, but I'm also just not much good wi' numbers. When I were at school, we 'ad to calculate pi to 15 decimal places. What a waste of time! The only pi I've ever worked out is steak and kidney, washed down with gallons of Yorkshire bitter. Now that's worth calculating!*

TWO GAGS

Gags are commonly used in the sado-masochism scene… apparently. But they're also handy if you want to remind both members of a cheating couple not to breathe a bloody word t'missus. For the sake of anonymity, we'll call her 'Pauline Prescott'. Here's a little fetish scenario involving Two Jags, two gags and a shag.

HOW TO DO IT: Simple really. The couple basically have sex any which way. But gags must be worn at all times. That way, they can train themselves not to let a dicky bird slip out when the missus is about. Each time they see each other, they'll be reminded that their little secret must remain just that.

PREZZA SAYS: Actually, it wasn't 'ard to keep a secret from the wife. No one can make head nor tail of owt I say anyroadupwards. I were deliverin' a speech once at a Trade Union conference, when some cheeky git stood up and shouted, 'Do you come with subtitles?' I told him to 'F' off, but luckily no one could understand what I'd said.

SLUMPY PUMPY

Dopey Prescott can doze off anywhere – during Commons debates, Party conference speeches or memorial services. Newspapers used to love running the pictures, until it happened so often it was no longer news. Here's a position requiring no effort whatsoever from the somnolent slug.

HOW TO DO IT: The ultimate indulgence for fat, lazy blokes everywhere, this involves the man, sitting in a chair, his head tilted back, snoring like an idling tractor as his mate seats herself astride him. The trick for her is to complete the act without waking the dormant buffoon. In the unhappy event that he IS roused from his slumber, he must blurt out, 'I were never asleep. I were only restin' me eyes!'

PREZZA SAYS: *The Tory papers always make out I sleep on t'job. Chuffin' rubbish! I always give 100 per cent during t'workin' week. That works out to about 24 per cent every day Monday to Thursday, and another 4 per cent on Fridays.*

POKEY CROQUET

Two men fight over a girl in this unusual variation of the toffs' game beloved of the Deputy Prime Minister and his highly paid cronies. Normally a round of croquet serves as a break from a gruelling day of loafing around Dorneywood at taxpayers' expense while pretending to run the country. But why not make things interesting – by instituting a top prize of a roll on the manicured lawn with a willing civil servant?

HOW TO DO IT: The rules of croquet are too complex to go into here. Suffice to say, it involves bashing balls through hoops using mallets until, as a thrilling finale, you have to strike a peg in the centre of the lawn. In this version, a bikini-clad aide (£60,000-a-year plus car and perks) basks in the sunshine as a lure for the chaps. The winner is treated to a romp in full view of photographers for a Sunday newspaper. The loser consoles himself by downing a bottle of State-funded wine under a tree.

PREZZA SAYS: *I got a lorra stick over the croquet. But it weren't my fault – it were some Tory toff what bought the set in the first place.*

And anyway, what normal bloke hasn't played with his balls during working hours? There isn't a law against it... is there?

PARK AND RIDE

John Prescott wants to tax drivers off the road and force them on to the bus. Only by doing this can he ensure the roads are clear for him to zip along in a chauffeur-driven Jag. Those rich enough to

defiantly persist with driving will pay £8 to go into a city, £15 to park, £60 if they stray over 30mph and £100 every time they fill up. If they take the train, they will pay £50 to go 40 miles at peak time. This money can then be ploughed into improving the lives of New Labour supporters or Cabinet Ministers. Here's an alternative manoeuvre for Prescott *aficionados*.

HOW TO DO IT: Priced off the road, the man and woman pay through the nose to park in a dimly lit wasteland frequented by car thieves and muggers before embarking on a cold, unlit double-decker smelling of urine. They take comfort by indulging in a passionate kiss and cuddle on the back seat. The certain knowledge that at any time they might be mugged and stabbed by a crack addict adds a thrilling extra risk to proceedings.

PREZZA SAYS: *Thanks to Labour and all t'improvements on public transport, motorists have a real choice for the first time – they can either bankrupt themselves in their cars or on the train. It's their choice.*

SHIVER ME TIMBERS

A colourful, swashbuckling frolic inspired by Prescott's movie preferences. 'I like things I want to enjoy,' he revealed with his usual eloquence. 'I like Westerns, I like pirates. I want to come out walking like John Wayne.' A desire seemingly shared by Tracey Temple, who regularly emerged from his flat walking like John Wayne after a day in the saddle.

HOW TO DO IT: The man, fully dressed as Long John Silver (or, in this case, Short Fat John Silver), swings into the room on a rope, a cutlass clenched between his teeth. With a hearty 'Arrrggghh, Jim lad', he whisks his partner off her feet and drags her to the corner for a knee-trembler.

PREZZA SAYS: *When I were a kid, I were playin' pirates with me mates, when they all ran off. My mum says to me, 'Hello, Mr Pirate, where are your buccaneers?' 'On the side of me buccin' 'ead, you daft moo,' I says.*

TOAD IN THE HOLE

A sign on a side door at Dorneywood says 'Toad Hall'. Of course, we cannot know whether the Prescotts put it there, but in the absence of evidence to the contrary – and in light of Prescott being the personification of Mr Toad – we will assume they did.

HOW TO DO IT: Best performed in a lakeside setting, or pond if easier, this involves the man leaping, toadlike, from a crouching position in pursuit of his mate. She must flee in similar fashion. Both must emit the sound 'ribbit, ribbit…'. It is, of course, best if the man is short and squat, to more accurately imitate both a toad and Prescott, if indeed there is a difference. Due to his superior strength, the male will invariably catch the female and an amphibious landing may take place.

PREZZA SAYS: *Mr Toad's my hero, he is. He's greedy, eats like a pig, drives a big car and lives in a big 'ouse. It were bloody unfair when they put 'im in jail and let them chuffin' weasels have Dorneywood… er… Toad Hall, I mean.*

CHAPTER FOUR

SEX GAMES

Variety is the spice of a great sex life. Here are some naughty positions beloved of the DPM.

VAST TANGO IN PARIS

Marlon Brando's influence on Prescott's life is unmistakable. For starters, they both became astonishingly fat. And the DPM considers Brando's *On the Waterfront* character sufficiently like him that he named the Oscar-winner as the man who should play him in the movie of his life. Where else, then,

could Prezza have turned for inspiration than to the infamous 'butter scene' in *Last Tango in Paris*?

HOW TO DO IT: Buy 4lbs butter (or lard). Go to empty flat. Meet strange woman. Remove clothes, lie on floor. Violently, before the woman has a chance to react, the man spreads the melting butter all over her naked form. Then, in a shocking display of carnal savagery, he licks every last ounce of it from her before collapsing, clutching his bulging belly with a satiated sigh. For extra calories, take a packet of digestives.

PREZZA SAYS: *Grub and sex 'av always gone together for me. Once I were in café lookin' at the menu, and the waitress said, 'What would ya like?' I winked at her and said, 'I'll 'av a quickie, luv.' She were shocked – and t'missus were bloody furious. 'It's "quiche", you oaf,' she said.*

PIG~~GY~~ IN THE MIDDLE

A kinky threesome inspired by Prescott's tenuous, and only, role in New Labour – keeping the peace between Gordon Brown on the Left and Tony Blair on the Right.

HOW TO DO IT: The man picks up two women involved in a vicious catfight. He takes them back to his place and beds them, with one on his left and the other on his right. The women detest each other and will never make peace, so in that sense it is not a genuine threesome. But hey, who's complaining?

PREZZA SAYS: *Yer just can't beat a threesome. It's not just for the sex, mind. It's 'cos ya can split the 'otel bill three ways instead o' two! Chuffin' genius, that is!*

THE DUNGEON MASTER

Helping the poor was Prescott's motivation for a life in politics. Odd, then, that he ended up presiding over council tax rises so objectionable that hard-up pensioners were prepared to go to jail rather than pay them. It is obviously scurrilous to suggest Prescott derived a thrill from such a result. So here goes.

HOW TO DO IT: This frankly disgraceful 'master and servant' position sees the man 'jailing' his partner for a trifling offence, such as being unable to pay an enormous tax he has unfairly demanded. As she languishes (naked, naturally) in his makeshift prison, our aroused 'jailer' sits counting huge piles of cash he has inexplicably been handed by taxpayers.

PREZZA SAYS: By 'eck, I must admit, everyone seems to 'ate me now. And I were never that popular to start with. Even when I were a kid, me mum and dad 'ad to tie a pork chop to me leg just to get the bleedin' dog to play wi' me.

THE BUM'S RUSH

Few Cabinet Ministers have ever deserved the bullet more than Prescott, what with the incessant stupidity and the shame he has heaped on his office. Here's a kinky scene perfect for a man in his precarious position.

HOW TO DO IT: Shame-faced, the man lowers his trousers, bends over and prepares for punishment. His partner, whip in hand, begins to flay his bare buttocks, saying thus: 'You've been a very naughty, sleazy, incompetent, greedy, selfish, money-grubbing, hypocritical, lecherous, ungrammatical and environ-mentally unsound boy. And did I mention the incompetence?'

PREZZA SAYS: *People 'av always been cruel to me 'cos I'm a bit slow. Someone used to ring me office phone asking me to get hold of members of me staff. I spent weeks running round my team asking for Seymour Butts and Homer Sexual. Once I had to ask everyone, 'Has anyone seen Mike Rotch?' The joke was on them, though, 'cos none of them people worked for me. Hah!*

A CLOWN CALLED MALICE

An apt scenario for the mean-spirited buffoon that is Prescott. It's inspired by The Jam's song 'A Town Called Malice' – a favourite number he claims to play on his iPod. Or, as he calls it, his 'Pie Pod'.

HOW TO DO IT: A clown, a custard pie, a scantily clad woman. Use your imagination.

PREZZA SAYS: *I don't like bein' called a clown, me. They say it teks 42 muscles to frown and only 28 to smile. Well, ya know what? It only teks four chuffin' muscles to swing me arm round and smack you in the gob!*

HEAVEN AND HULL

In the city of Hull, where there's muck, there's brass – and they don't come much brassier or muckier than Prescott. Because of this, he is a huge figure up North… and in the South, East and West, too, for that matter. Locals have afforded him cult status, and will turn a blind eye to the worst of his excesses, as long as he nips back to his homestead to favour the minions with a wave, a cheesy grin, and the scattering of a few pennies among the poor. And, as long as there are a few paparazzi around to capture Prezza rubbing shoulders with the serfs, everyone's happy. And no one likes pressing the flesh more than the Right Honourable Member for Hull East.

HOW TO DO IT: Buy a huge house in Hull. This should cost no more than a few quid. With a few hundred pounds, you can take control of a large area of the city. From the gated confines of your stately home, keep an eye on wedding announcements in the local press. Come each couple's Big Day, you can exercise your feudal rights. Not, we hasten to add, that Prezza's ever done this. But he's missed a trick there!

PREZZA SAYS: *I've always been very loyal to me 'ome town, like. Once I were in a car crash. I were covered in blood, and the ambulance bird says to me, 'Where are you bleeding from?' 'I'm from bleedin' 'Ull,' I says, 'an' right proud of it 'n' all.'*

MINISTER WITHOUT BRIEFS

A roleplaying fantasy. After proving incompetent in Government – and then humiliating his office with a sex scandal – Prescott was stripped of all his briefs. Mind you, he kept his entire package of pay and perks, losing only the use of one of his three homes.

HOW TO DO IT: The man must enter a room and stand, head bowed, before a desk, behind which sits his stern-faced lover. She puts on a Tony Blair mask and, like a lion stalking its prey, prowls around her helpless mate, mercilessly stripping him one by one of his clothes and his dignity. Humiliated, the naked man must crawl on all fours before her, apologising.

PREZZA SAYS: *This is the life – 'avin' nowt to do. When I were at school, we had to write an essay on what we'd do if we won a million quid. I 'anded in a blank sheet o' paper. Teacher says, 'Ayup, John, you've done nowt.' I says, 'Yep, and that's what I'll do if I get rich!' And chuffin' 'ell… it's all come true!*

SLAVE OF THE UNION

Trade Union blood runs through Prescott's veins. He entered politics as a union delegate in the 1960s and spent 47 years in the RMT. Even now that he's meant to act like a statesman, the DPM barrels about like a belligerent little shop steward.

HOW TO DO IT: This kinky S&M position sees the naked man lying prone on the floor as a whiplash-wielding Dominatrix towers above him wearing a flat-cap and holding a whippet on a string. For full effect, slogans must be placed around the room on placards, such as 'MANAGEMENT STINKS' and 'DOWN WITH BOURGEOIS BASTARDS'. The participants must resist the temptation to call each other 'mistress' or 'slave'; only 'comrade' is appropriate.

PREZZA SAYS: *I were always fond of t'union, me. Shoutin', swearin' and stickin' one over the evil boss... but Pauline got used to it eventually. Then I became a boss meself, and now I've got stripped of me assets, I've got a good mind to go on strike. Trouble is, no one will notice.*

NATIONAL YOLK

Here's a truly revolting game inspired by Prescott's infamous decking of an egg-chucker during the 2001 election campaign. Most politicians can take a yolk or two. Not Prescott, whose indignation erupted into a display of violence which disgraced his office and which would have earned lesser mortals an assault conviction. Prezza kept his clean criminal record and his job.

HOW TO DO IT: Only for the most broad-minded and consenting adults prepared for a large dry-cleaning bill, this game involves the man, fully suited, being pelted with eggs. In seconds, he must erupt into a Prescottesque fury before grappling his partner to the ground. Actually landing a right hook to the jaw is not advised, though it would be in keeping with the game's inspiration. Eventually, the couple slither playfully around in a sea of eggs and shells and further intimacy may follow.

An additional bonus is that a huge omelette can be enjoyed during or after coitus.

PREZZA SAYS: *All reet, I confess, I do 'av a bit of a short fuse. Once, I were driving down a* *country road when a woman coming towards me shouts out of her window, 'Pig!' I were furious. I shouts back, 'Bitch!' A couple of minutes later, I went round a corner and hit a huge porker stood right in middle of road. I couldn't bloody believe it. Mind you, I still don't know why that bitch called me a pig.*

SILLY SAUSAGE

Prescott hates journalists – especially when they ask questions that undermine whatever PR stunt he's trying to foist on the public that day. His weapon is humiliation. Want to ask about his three homes? You're a 'silly girl'. The gas-guzzling Jags? You're 'daft'. A defecting Labour MP? 'You're an amateur, mate!' So here's a kinky game where the journalists get their own back.

HOW TO DO IT: The man is prostrate on the floor, naked. The woman, fully clothed, with trilby on head and press card in the hat band, walks all over the bloke with her stilettos until he is begging for mercy. After ten minutes of torture, he has renounced his Jags, given up the grace-and-favour homes and agreed to stand down at the next election. Another triumph for a campaigning press.

PREZZA SAYS: Some people do ask bloody silly questions. T'other day, some bird from me bank rang up and asked for me date o' birth. 'May 31st,' I says. 'What year?' she asks. 'Every bloody year!' I says. Silly cow.

ORDER OF THE BATH

As he proved when Tony Blair trusted him with various Departments of State, John Prescott couldn't run a bath. Nevertheless, he decided to run OUR baths – with a new edict limiting the temperature of our hot water. Troubled by an apparent increase in scaldings, the meddling moron decided he alone was the man to take control of this most private area of our lives.

HOW TO DO IT: Light the candles, fire up some seductive music and break out the aromatherapy oils for a sensuous night of bathtime lovemaking… with a twist. As SHE slips beneath the bubbles and the tub fills with steaming hot water, HE enters the room, disrobes and prepares to join her. Dipping his toe, he must then suddenly exclaim, 'Bleedin' Nora, ya daft moo – d'ya know what 'ealth and safety would say about water this chuffin' hot?' He must then turn the cold tap on full. Sex will ensue as the couple must now huddle together in the lukewarm water to keep warm.

PREZZA SAYS: *Scaldin' is the biggest crisis facing bath users today. My legacy to this*

Government's period of office is to have made Britain's bathtime safer. When Britons step into their tepid baths, I know they'll be thanking me for having a hand in their tubs.

CHAPTER FIVE

PLEASING YOURSELF

Sometimes, even the charms of a disgraced Deputy Prime Minister are simply not enough to attract a willing sexual partner. Incredible as it sounds, a gurning tub of lard from one of the whiffiest cities in the British Isles has to accept that the opposite sex does sometimes have eyes, ears and a desire to run screaming from the room. Such is increasingly the case for John Prescott. When all else fails, matters must then be taken into your own hand.

SNOOP DOGGER

John likes 'to watch'. He particularly likes to watch your conservatory. Or your garden. Or your view over the countryside. Let us explain – the DPM hates the middle class, with their fancy-pants house extensions, nice views and swanky loft conversions. So he figures it's only right and proper these privileged folk should pay through the nose for improving their homes – by shifting them up into a dearer council tax bracket. And he has accordingly equipped his inspectors to snoop on us all with zoom lenses.

HOW TO DO IT: A solo sex act perfect for the frustrated class warrior needing instant relief from a bout of envy. Find a nice suburb with sparkling 4x4s on each drive and make camp in a well-trimmed hedgerow. As darkness falls, extract your binoculars for a close-up view of opulent uPVC conservatories and luxurious double-glazing. Leave one hand free for sexual release!

PREZZA SAYS: Them public school Tory voters born with silver spoons in their mouths really get up me nose. I know what it's like to

be poor, me. We used to keep coal in the bath. Now I'm second-in-command, I keeps it in the bidet. Which makes it bloody 'ard to wash me bum, I can tell yer.

THE VOYEUR

While employing the same principle as 'Snoop Dogger' (see previous entry), this position is perfect for those who enjoy such activity in the privacy of their own home and in front of a computer. Handily, Prescott intends for his tax snoopers to post pictures of people's homes and their values on the Internet, thus enabling their master to look at them at his leisure.

HOW TO DO IT: Call up the Government website set up for this very purpose. Search for homes in your neighbourhood and ogle the neighbour's magnificent plastic car port – worthy, surely, of the Palace of Versailles and certainly a perfect excuse to increase the owner's tax bill.

PREZZA SAYS: *I bloody love t'Internet. You can nick a speech on environmental damage control so much quicker than you ever could before, and it leaves loads of time for more important things, like smackin' them big balls round a croquet green. I don't reckon much to online banking though. I've put me PIN number in loads of times, but I can never find the slot where the money comes out.*

TRUE GIT

What was Two Jags doing on the 32,000-acre Colorado ranch of the billionaire who wants the Government to let him open a super-casino at the Dome? Why, yee-haw and fiddle-dee-dee! He was innocently experiencing the Wild West, like the cowboy heroes of the Westerns he loves. And, as Clint Eastwood once said, 'If you believe that, I got some swamp land for ya.'

HOW TO DO IT: This appalling position combines two of Prescott's great loves, lassoing and women. The male, in stetson, denim and chaps, a six-shooter on his hip and his horse buckling beneath him, canters around the corral as he lassoes the scantily clad object of his gunslinger's lust. After roping her, he turns her over like a steer ready for branding, before making her his. Now that sure is one lucky cowgirl, eh, Prezza?

PREZZA SAYS: *Giddy up! Heh heh! I love them Westerns, me. I always wanted t'ride a big 'orse and feel summat warm and powerful 'tween me legs for once. I specially love that one, Fistful o' Dollars – reminds me o' me pay* cheque! In fact, t'only reason I agreed to become Tony's dep-tee in the first place was 'cos I thought he were a sheriff getting up a posse. How were I ter know he were bloody Prime Minister?

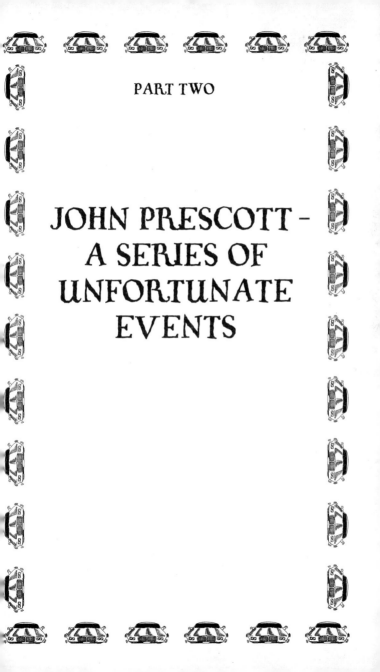

PART TWO

JOHN PRESCOTT - A SERIES OF UNFORTUNATE EVENTS

Laughter and sex go together like port and stilton, bacon and eggs… or John Prescott and a willing diary secretary. And when you're on the job with Prezza, there's guaranteed laughter all the way – and not all of it is intentional. Lord knows, it's tough being the Deputy Prime Minister, particularly when you put your foot in your mouth as often as Prezza. Most of us would get away with a gaffe or two, but he has a knack for committing outrageous blunders in public, and often with a few journalists and paparazzi in tow for good measure.

It is impossible to list here a complete record of the great man's blunders – the finished book would weigh even more than he does – so we'll confine ourselves to the most significant events that have befallen the Deputy Prime Minister as recounted by friends, family, colleagues and, of course, former squeezes. All or some of the following are no doubt fictional, and names have been changed to protect the innocent from having their lights punched out by several hundredweight of prime Hull beef.

The intricacies of the Kama Sutra, Prescott-style, don't come easily. They have to be worked at, honed, caressed and nurtured, until lovemaking transcends the ordinary, and becomes an act of pure heaven on earth... or just lasts longer than the regulation three-and-a-half minutes.

After their fabulous wedding, friends of the Prescotts tell us that John and Pauline went on honeymoon to a swanky hotel on a paradise island. They went up to the reception and mentioned that they'd booked a suite.

'Bridal?' asked the receptionist.

'Oh no, don't worry,' replied Prezza, 'she'll just grab hold of me shoulders and I'll bang away until we get the hang of it.'

It's not widely known that the current Member of Parliament for Hull East was a regular sperm donor when he was younger, but stopped donating just before he was elected to Parliament. A former receptionist at the sperm bank recalls that Prezza wandered into the centre one afternoon, and announced, 'I'd like ter make a donation, luv...'

'Certainly, sir,' the receptionist replied, 'have you donated before?'

'Yup,' Prezza grinned. 'You should have me details on yer computer.'

'Oh yes, I've found your records,' said the receptionist, 'but I see you're going to need help. Shall I call your wife for you?'

'Why do I need 'elp?' asked the future Deputy Prime Minister.

'Well, Mr Prescott, it says here that you're a useless wanker...'

A housekeeper of the Prescotts says that she witnessed Pauline and John sitting in front of the television at Dorneywood watching the six o'clock news. The main story was about a man threatening to jump off the Clifton Suspension Bridge.

Pauline turned to her husband and said, 'John, I bet you £5,000 that he jumps!' To which Prezza replied, '£5,000? Done! I bet that he doesn't.'

So they shake hands on the bet and continue watching. Sure enough, the man jumped and hit the ground below with a loud thud. So Prezza went to the huge tankard on the mantelpiece, counted out £5,000 in fifties, and grudgingly handed over the wad to Pauline.

But she refused. 'I can't take the taxpayers' money, John,' she says. 'The truth is, I was cheating. I caught the lunchtime news, so I knew he was going to jump.'

'Aw, fair's fair, trout-face,' said Prezza.

The same housekeeper recalls that, when Pauline announced to John that she was pregnant with their first child, he was obviously thrilled.

'That's smashin',' he said. 'We'd better get down t'supermarket sharpish.'

'Why do we need to go to the supermarket, honey-bunch?' asked Pauline.

Prezza rolled his eyes in despair. 'Because they have free delivery.'

Having finally been elected as Member of Parliament for Kingston Upon Hull East, Prezza decided that it was time to buy a well-to-do house in the constituency, as he was now moving rapidly up in the world. But he still wanted to be seen to be staying close to his working-class roots, so he decided to do some of the DIY himself – which included painting his new front door.

Neighbours report that, one hot summer's day, Pauline came back from the shops to find her rotund hubby applying some red gloss paint to the front door.

'You're doing a great job, Big Bollocks,' she said. 'But tell me, why are you wearing your grey leather bomber jacket and your raincoat?'

The new Member of Parliament sighed to himself and pointed at the tin. 'It says 'ere, "For best results, put on two coats".'

On one of his official visits as Deputy Leader, it was reported that Prezza visited a school in his Hull constituency. In one class, he thought he'd educate the boys and girls in the art of political diplomacy, so he asked the students if anyone could give him an example of a 'tragedy'.

One boy stood up and said, 'If my best friend who lives next door was playing in the street, and a car came along and killed him, that would be a tragedy.'

'No,' Prezza said, 'that would be an ACCIDENT.'

A girl raised her hand. 'If a school bus carrying 50 children drove off a cliff, killing everyone involved, that would be a tragedy.'

'I'm afraid not,' explained Prezza. 'That is what we would call a GREAT LOSS.'

The room went silent, as none of the children felt capable of answering the great man's question.

'Come on, kids,' said Prezza. 'Isn't there anyone here who can give me an example of a tragedy?'

Finally, a boy in the back raised his hand. In a timid voice, he said, 'If you were on a plane, and it was blown up by a bomb, that would be a tragedy.'

Prezza's round face beamed with delight. 'Flippin' marvellous! And can you tell me WHY that would be a tragedy?'

'Well,' said the boy, 'because it wouldn't be an accident and it certainly wouldn't be a great loss.'

Prezza famously went shopping and saw something interesting in the kitchen department of a large store.

'What's that?' he asked an assistant.

'A Thermos flask,' she replied.

'What's it do?' the big-bellied Parliamentarian asked.

The assistant told him it keeps hot things hot, and cold things cold.

Really impressed, Prezza thought it would be really handy for his long trips between London and Hull in his Jag, so he bought one and tried it out on his next trip South. Really proud of his gleaming purchase, he showed it off to his chauffeur.

''Ere, 'Enry, look at this beauty...' he said proudly.

'Mmmm... looks lovely, gaffer...' said the driver, clearly a little underwhelmed.

'It's a Thermos flask,' continued Prezza, 'it keeps hot things hot, and cold things cold.'

'That sounds wonderful, sir,' said the chauffeur, 'what have you got in it?'

'Two cups of coffee and a choc ice,' said our Member for Hull East.

When Prezza took possession of his first Jag, he couldn't resist taking it for a spin to show it off to Pauline. He was happily putting the powerful beast through its paces, when he noticed a flashing blue light in the rear-view mirror. He pulled over and a policeman approached the car.

'I thought you ought to know, sir, that there is a woman about a mile back who claims to be your wife. She says she fell out of the car when you turned a corner.'

'Thank God for that,' said Prezza. 'I thought I'd gone deaf.'

Not so long ago, Prezza decided to test drive one of the latest Jaguars to see if it was sufficiently ministerial, so he wedged himself behind the steering wheel and set off with Pauline alongside him. He hadn't gone very far before the flashing blue light in the rear-view mirror alerted Prezza to even more police interest. Annoyed, he pulled over, convinced that he had done nothing wrong.

'Afternoon, officer,' the tubby driver grinned. 'What's the matter?'

'I'm a little curious, sir,' the policeman replied. 'You have been travelling at four miles an hour. Is everything all right?'

'Fine, officer,' he replies, 'It's just that t'sign back there says that t'speed limit was four miles per hour...'

'Er, no,' said the policeman, 'that's not the speed limit, that's the name of the road. You're on the M4.'

At this point, the traffic cop looked across to the passenger seat and noticed Pauline looking white as a sheet, trembling, with her white-knuckled hands gripping the dashboard in front of her.

'**What's wrong with her?**' asked the policeman.

'**Oh nothing,**' answered Prezza a little sheepishly. '**We just came off the A316...**'

Prezza has always had hassle with his cars, whether it's because of his driving, his choice of petrol-guzzling Jags or the backlash from driving a couple of hundred yards to safeguard Pauline's hairdo. Cars and Prezza simply don't mix.

On one occasion, a member of staff at Dorneywood recalls a thief driving off with Prezza's new, top-of-the-range Jag. It was all witnessed by the Deputy Prime Minister himself, who ran from the bedroom down the vast staircase shouting, 'Pauline, Pauline, some bastard's just driven off with me car.'

'Oh my God,' Pauline shouted,

running out from the kitchen. 'Did you get a description of him?'

'I did better than that,' said the Deputy PM triumphantly, brandishing a scrap of paper. 'I managed to write down the number plate!'

In order to find favour with a critical public, who have not always been very complimentary about his two-Jag status, Prezza has attempted to travel to several official engagements on the train, although this is fraught with danger.

On one occasion, a train guard remembers approaching the Member for Hull East and asking him for his ticket. Prezza searched his pockets in an increasing state of agitation and finally admitted, 'Oh bugger it...

Look, pal, I must have lost me bloody ticket.'

'Don't worry about it, Mr

Prescott,' the guard said. 'I'm sure you're not a fare dodger.'

'You don't understand,' replied Prezza, the veins standing out on his temple, 'Ah've got ter find it... otherwise I won't know where t'get off!'

When the Prescotts moved into their grace-and-favour country pile, Dorneywood, the Deputy Prime Minster was invited by some wealthy local neighbours to join them on a shooting trip on a nearby estate. Before going, our new Lord of the Manor went to a very expensive shop and bought all the gear, then set out in his Jag, gun at the ready.

In the heart of the countryside, before he arrived at his destination, he spied a plump, juicy-looking pheasant in a field. He stopped the car, got out his gun and blew it to smithereens. Just as he was picking up his pheasant, a farmer appeared.

'That'll be my bird you just shot,' he said.

'What d'ya mean?' asked the reddening Deputy Prime Minister. 'I shot it.'

'But it was on my land. I'll tell you what, we'll settle this the way we settle all disputes round here. I'll give you a good kick in your knackers, you do the same to me, and whoever's still standing can keep the pheasant.'

'Fair enough,' said Prezza, confident of his pain threshold.

'OK then,' said the farmer. 'I'll go first.'

With that, he took a long run-up, and kicked our Member for Hull East as hard as he could smack bang in the crown jewels. There was a crunching sound as Prezza doubled over in pain, but just about remained standing.

'UUU-uuu-uuuuuh... OK,' he gasped, barely able to breathe, his voice several octaves higher. 'My turn.'

'Oh, don't worry about it, Mr Prescott,' said the farmer. 'You keep the pheasant.'

A Cabinet colleague recalled the day a new member of the admin team was shown around the office of the Deputy Prime Minister, just before a Cabinet briefing. The entire team was present, with Prezza holding centre stage. The new assistant, Mischa from the Ukraine, was introduced to everyone by the Director of Admin Support, who explained that Mischa would be working in the office for the next few weeks.

The Director went on to say, 'Now that we have got that sorted out, let me explain some basics... we call this a "pen",' as she held up a ballpoint pen, 'and this is "paper" that you sometimes have to sign.

This is a "desk", and that big box thing over there with the moving lights is a "computer"...'

At this point, the new assistant politely interrupted his new boss. 'Forgive me, but I've lived in the UK for several years, I went to Oxford and am very familiar with the English language...'

The Director replied, 'I know that, Mischa... I was talking to the Deputy Prime Minister.'

Having found that his stomach stopped him from standing close enough to a lectern to read a speech, Prezza decided that enough was enough – he had to lose some weight. So he hurriedly appointed a personal trainer, who got down to business immediately.

'What I want you to do,' he said, 'is eat normally for three days then skip a day. Carry that on for a month, and then come back to see me.'

Sure enough, a month later the former human bowling ball came back looking much leaner and fitter.

'That's a flippin' magic diet,' Prezza said, 'but you know, I thought I were going to drop dead every fourth day.'

'What from?' asked the trainer. 'Hunger?'

'No,' said our Hull hunk, 'from skipping.'

Naturally, as part of his official duties, the Deputy Prime Minister and his wife are often invited out to fancy receptions, parties, openings, premières and so on. And, when one or two pints hit the back of the Prescott throat, several more are bound to follow. And there's nothing that makes a man from Hull more frisky than a few sherries and several pints of bitter.

One evening, several passers-by noticed Prezza staggering about on a pavement in the West End, completely pissed, with a key in his hand. A policeman was alerted, and he approached the reeling Cabinet Minister.

'What's going on 'ere then?' asked the copper.

'They shtole me bloody car!' shouted Prezza.

'Where did you last see it?' asked the copper.

'On t'end of thish key!' Prezza wailed.

The policeman looked him up and down and moved closer to whisper in Prezza's ear, 'Are you aware, sir, that your penis is poking out of your trousers?'

'Aaaaw... shit!' screamed the Deputy PM. 'They got Pauline as well!'

PART THREE

GIT OF THE GAB - PRESCOTT'S TEN FAVOURITE CHAT-UP LINES

'You remind me of me constituency, 'Ull East – you're ugly and you whiff a bit, but I'll go there if I 'av to.'

''Ow about it, luv? I make brass from taxpayers faster than you could spend it.'

'Me name's Prescott. John Prescott, Deputy Prime Minister, First Secretary of State and MP for 'Ull East. That's so you know what name to scream out tonight.'

'Let's 'av breakfast tomorrow. Should I call ya... or nudge ya?'

'I 'av the brains of Fred Flintstone – I bet I can make your bed rock!'

'I may not be t'best-lookin' guy in the world, bur I'm t'only chuffin' Deputy Prime Minister you'll ever pull.'

'Ayup, love. Do ya want ter see some magic? We nip up to me grace-and-favour flat, shag... then you disappear!'

'You don't sweat much for a fat lass.'

'I'm not really this tall.
I'm sittin' on all t'brass
taxpayers give me.'

'Ayup, luv, 'ow about free
lunch at Commons, then a
shag? No? Oh, all right,
just the shag then.'

PART FOUR

THE BUTT
STOPS HERE

TEN JOHN PRESCOTT JOKES

In his retirement, Prescott decides to farm chickens. He buys 100 chickens but they all die. He goes back to the dealer and gets another 100. They all die, too. He goes back to the dealer again and says, 'Ayup, I reckon I know where I'm going wrong now. I'm planting the buggers too deep!'

One day, Prescott is walking along a river bank when a bloke across the water shouts to him, 'Excuse me, sir – how do I get to the other side?' Prescott shouts back, 'You daft bugger, you *are* on the other side.'

Life is full of coincidences for John Prescott. 'For starters,' he says, 'me mam and dad got married the same day.'

Prescott went to the library and borrowed a book titled *How to Hug*. When he got home, he realised it was Volume 14 of the *Oxford English Dictionary*.

Prescott has the hots for a sexy young secretary. She tells him with a wink, 'Call round tomorrow – no one will be at home.' So next day he calls round at her place. No one there.

Unusually, Prescott is reading a book. After three days, he gives up and tells his wife, 'There are too many characters and I can't make head or tail of the plot.' 'You daft oaf,' says his missus. 'That's the phone book.'

As a child, Prescott came home and delightedly told his parents, 'I got 100 per cent in the school tests.' 'Really?' said his dad, incredulously. 'Yes,' says dim-witted John. '25 per cent in maths, 35 in science, 30 in geography and 10 in English.'

Why does John Prescott weep during sex? CS gas will do that to you.

Why does John Prescott hate chocolate oranges? They're devilishly hard to peel.

Why are Prescott jokes so short? So even an idiot like him can understand them!

PREZZA'S TOP TEN GAGS

Why is a Wonder Bra called a Wonder Bra?
'Cos when she takes it off, you wonder where her chuffin' boobs went!

How many men does it take to open a beer bottle?
None! It should be open when the chuffin' missus brings it to ya.

Why is t'space between a woman's breasts and her 'ips called a waist? 'Cos you could easily fit another pair of boobs in there!

What do you do when yer missus comes out of kitchen to nag yer? Shorten her bloody chain!

What's the difference between a bachelor and a married bloke? Bachelor comes home, sees what's in the fridge, goes to bed. Married man comes home, sees what's in bed, goes t'fridge. I do, anyroad.

Why are hangovers better than women? A hangover will go away!

Why do brides always wear white? To match the chuffin' kitchen appliances!

***What's worse than a male chauvinist pig?
A chuffin' woman who won't do
what she's told!***

***What do you call an unmarried
woman in a BMW?
A blinkin' divorcee!***

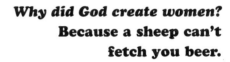

***Why did God create women?
Because a sheep can't
fetch you beer.***

PART FIVE

HE'S HISTORY- PREZZA AS TEN ~~GREAT~~ SHA~~GG~~ERS OF THE PAST

RUDE OAF VALENTINO

How the history of cinema would have changed if Prezza had been the first great sex symbol of the silver screen. Although he would definitely have had to be shot in widescreen format.

CRASSANOVA

Lumpen Prezza has much in common with the 6ft 3ins 18th-century Venetian dandy – well, they both had two arms and two legs.

RED BUTLER

Leftie Prescott makes a perfect Rhett – his career's gone with the wind. And frankly, my dears, he doesn't give a damn.

HUMPTY BOGART

Imagine *Casablanca* with Prezza as Bogart's bitter romantic Rick. Ingrid Bergman would have taken one look at him and fled the bar in disgust.

HENRY THE ATE

Gluttony, greed, shagging – yes, there's much to link Prezza with the notorious monarch. Like Henry, he even has a Tudor mansion. Well, mock-Tudor at any rate.

THE PIE WHO LOVED ME

What were they thinking casting Daniel Craig as Bond? Prescott was born to play him… in *For Your Pies Only*, *Live and Let Pie*, *Pie Another Day* and *GoldenPie*.

ROLLMEO

He's fat, he's round, he rolls along the ground, as William Shakespeare would have written had he thought of it. Prezza would have made an unusual suitor for young Juliet – and the balcony would never have taken his weight.

SHAME WARNE

Both like to get their leg over. Only one can turn his arm over.

HUGE HEFNER

Prescott's dream – a vast mansion and a bevy of gorgeous playmates.

FLABBA THE HUTT

OK, the *Star Wars* gangster's not exactly a swordsman. Unless you count the slave girls. But you've got to admit the resemblance is uncanny.

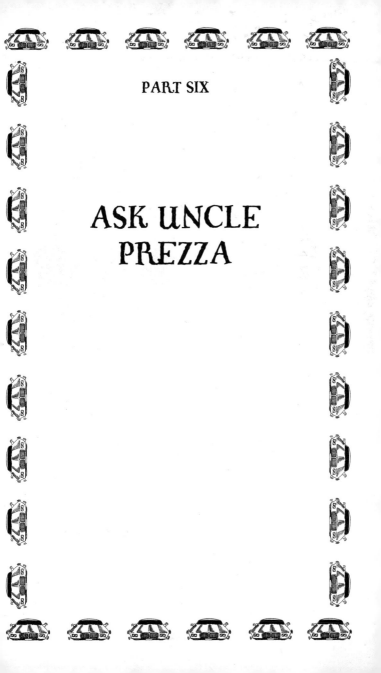

PART SIX

ASK UNCLE PREZZA

With a lifetime combining sexual and emotional experience with a career at the highest levels of Government, John Prescott is ideally placed to become Britain's number-one Agony Uncle. Here, he answers 20 typical questions all agony columnists receive. His advice may be uncompromising... inflexible... moronic. But he might just save your relationship.

DEAR PREZZA,

My son has had a really tough few years as a teenager. His dad left us and he had to be the father figure to my youngest children. It's given him a terrible temper. He flies off the handle all the time and frankly I'm a bit scared of him. He's a great kid, really — I just want him to come out of this phase and become the good man I know he could be.

Margaret Tickworth
Cheltenham

PREZZA SAYS:

Your son is angry and upset over your husband walking out, and understandably so. What he needs now is a RIGHT BLOODY THICK EAR. Little sod, throwing his weight around like a playground bully. Who does he think he is, anyroad… Deputy Prime Minister? We should bring back National bloody Service for little hooligans like 'im. What he needs is a chuffin' ASBO. That'll sort him. Hope this helped.

Prezza

DEAR PREZZA,

I need more variety in my sex life. My boyfriend is only happy in one position – with me on top – and claims he struggles to become aroused any other way. What can I do to encourage him to be a bit more adventurous?

Doreen Appleby
Little Gaddesdon

PREZZA SAYS:

Nowt, love. He's just a lazy bleeder. Reminds me o' me! Heh, heh! No seriously, though, it's not that he doesn't care, it's just that he can't be arsed doin' owt to please ya. Surely you can understand that? You'll have to be tough, mind, if yer want to sort it out. If he won't – pardon my French – roger you in any other way, give him the big E and find someone who will. I'm sending you a free advice leaflet with me mobile number on it.

Prezza

DEAR PREZZA,

I've been married for a long time now and have always suspected my husband had a wandering eye but I never thought he would stray. Although he's a powerful man and attractive to starstruck young girls, he's fat and rather slow on the uptake. Recently I've begun to wonder, though. There's a spring in his step. And I certainly haven't put it there.

Deidre Buxton
Stoke on Trent

PREZZA SAYS:

You're a right bloody suspicious old moo, you. All sorts of things can put a 'spring in t' step' of a fat dimwit. A plate of egg and chips, for starters. And another plate for main course an' all! Anyway, sounds like he'd be better off with some young tart than a crochety old cow like you.

Prezza

DEAR PREZZA,

My best friend's husband is cheating on her and I am torn apart over whether to tell her. We've known each other so long but I worry about the damage I'll do if I let on. Her husband's a good-looking guy and I suspect he's had plenty of affairs on the quiet. But is my friend better off not knowing – after all, she seems happy enough in their relationship – and apart from his flings he treats her well.

Marjorie Spatchcock
Heaton Moor, Stockport

PREZZA SAYS:

This is what we in the agony game call a right bloody tricky question. On one hand you stand to upset yer mate if ya tell 'er. On t'other, you stand to gerra shag off her bloke if ya don't. All things tekken into account, I reckon ya keep schtum – but tell her bloke you want regular rumpo off of him to keep quiet. If he's got money, even better! That way, everyone's 'appy. She don't know owt, he don't get rumbled, and you get some action and free dosh to boot. My two favourites!

Prezza

DEAR PREZZA,

I really love my fiancée. We've been together a long time and we have two young kids we both dote on. But recently she's become really snappy. So much so that it's affecting our lives in a big way. I briefly considered leaving, but it would tear our kids apart. And it wouldn't be fair on my fiancée. I really want our relationship to last. What should I do to work it out?

Gerry Pooley
East Kirkbride

PREZZA SAYS:

Get out now, for chuff's sake. Nothing bloody worse than some whinin' woman. It's not enough that yer out at work all day so they can 'ave a nice 'ouse. Oh no! It's just 'Why haven't ya done this, John…?' 'Why 'aven't ya done that…?' You can always explain it t' kids later on. They'll understand – especially ya lad when he's growed up. He'll find out about bloody women for himself soon enough, anyroad.

Prezza

DEAR PREZZA,

I'm 17 and want to start having sex, but I'm worried about the size of my manhood. When it's aroused, it's the size of a chipolata sausage. When it's unaroused, it's tricky to see it at all. I've had a few girlfriends but I've stopped short of having sex because I'm worried they'll laugh at me. Is there anything I can do?

Julian Minto
Little Barkworth, Suffolk

PREZZA SAYS:

I'm the owner of a chipolata myself, son, so tek it from me there is nowt you can do to mek it bigger. Believe me, I've tried! But remember this – there's a lot more to pulling power than 'avin a big todger. Women find all manner o' things sexy – money, power and cars to name but two. My advice is to stand for Parliament right away. Try the Tories – they'll be in next. You could be in the Cabinet in five years – and you'll be beatin' birds off with a stick.

Prezza

DEAR PREZZA,

I met this hunky older man on a drunken night out and slept with him. We have carried on the relationship for weeks. He keeps inviting me over, cooking me dinner and sleeping with me but he won't commit to me enough even to let me stay the night. There's an age gap of nearly 20 years between us. I am starting to worry that I am being used.

Mary Sykes
Upper Slaughter

PREZZA SAYS:

You're STARTING to worry? Ya daft cow. Of course you're bein' bloody used. But what's wrong with that? He gets what he wants — a legover — and you get a free dinner. That's been t'deal between man and woman since dawn o' bloody time. This in't a problem at all if yer ask me — I dunno why you've written in, to be honest.

Prezza

DEAR PREZZA,

I have a well-paid job and a lovely big house but I'm so unhappy. I work long hours and have no time for a social life. I haven't had a girlfriend for two years but if I'm not working 14 hours a day my boss goes berserk. My friends envy the lifestyle they think I have – but they have no idea what the truth is.

Norman Jackson
Poole, Dorset

PREZZA SAYS:

Aye, you've painted yerself into a corner there, lad. I know how ya feel, though, like… I've got loads of money and a great big 'ouse, too. Difference is, I don't 'av ta work 14 hours a day fer it. Fourteen minutes would be overdoing it! The secret is my boss can't get rid o' me without getting the push himself. So I got away with bein' rubbish at whatever they gave me ta do. Finally, they took me job off me altogether… but kept payin' me! Bloody marvellous it is. Anyroad, that's enough about me for a few seconds. As for you … sorry, son, you're screwed.

Prezza

DEAR PREZZA,

When I was a teenager, I was seduced by the girl next door – and we ended up having regular sex for a couple of years. But she was always telling me to hurry up so we wouldn't get caught. That was 15 years ago. But quickies became such a habit that now I never seem to last very long. It's very frustrating. My girlfriend's very understanding but I know she feels let down.

Charles Markworth-Smythe
Butterfield, Norfolk

PREZZA SAYS:

Aye, I know all about this. It's called premature educalation. Used to 'av it meself, in fact. But now I can go a full minute, so all's well. Some blokes last longer by thinking of inanimate objects like sheds and wheelbarrers. No good for me, mind – I get too excited thinking about people's conservatories and car-ports and the like. I think o' Margaret Beckett instead. That seems to dull me sensitivity down below.

Prezza

DEAR PREZZA,

My life feels so empty since my wife left. I've lost the will to live and am thinking about ending it all. We met at school and were together 20 years. We had two beautiful kids but we grew apart and she finally walked out a year ago. She seems to have moved on – but I can't seem to let her go. On top of everything, I've lost my job.

Tony Coddling
Sellafield

PREZZA SAYS:

Listen, mate, I feel for ya, I really do. I felt pretty grim meself when Tony said I'd to move out o' Dorneywood. That were a bloody bad day, I can tell thee. The wife were furious. We only had two 'omes left! Still, I dusted meself down and got on with whatever it is I do. Not that you'll be able to do that, mind. What with 'aving no money, an' all. So maybe you're right – toppin' yerself might be the best bet. I'm sending you my free self-help leaflet, 'Toppin' Yerself'. Best o' luck.

Prezza

DEAR PREZZA,

I've been having terrible nightmares since I was a child. They're not about anything in particular – and I don't remember them in the morning anyway. But I hardly ever get a good night's sleep and it's making me irritable at home and at work. Is there anything I can do?

Maureen Pinkerton
West Hampstead

PREZZA SAYS:

Don't tell me about bloody nightmares! Can you imagine the night's kip I 'ad when I found out the chuffin' press 'ad the story about me an' Tracey Temple? It were bloody murder. Anyroad, what I recommend if you're missin' out on shut-eye is a sustained bout of heavy drinking. Funnily enough, the more ya drink, the better ya sleep. May not help with the irritability in the mornin', mind.

Prezza

DEAR PREZZA,

My wife is always moaning about the amount of football I watch. Footie is my world – but she just doesn't get it. I love her but we argue constantly. Just recently I met a nice girl at work who's mad about the beautiful game. She's married, but she's not happy either and has hinted we should get together. Would it solve any of my problems to have an affair with her?

Charlie Truckle
Tranmere

PREZZA SAYS:

Too bloody right it would. Life's too short to saddle yerself with a moaning Minnie who don't like the footie. This other bird sounds a better bet all round. You'd get footie AND shaggin'. Mind you, a relationship is about compromise. So tell yer cow of a missus you'll give her one last chance if she gets her bloody priorities right. Otherwise – to use an old football phrase – if she thinks it's all over, it will be, then.

Prezza

DEAR PREZZA,

I can't stand walking past mirrors because I'm convinced I'm ugly. I've put on a lot of weight in the two years since my girlfriend left. Plus, I have a real problem with spots and I'm losing my hair. It's really getting me down.

Barry Spudling
Hindhead, Surrey

PREZZA SAYS:

My 'eart goes out to ya, it really does. I can't imagine what you're going through, obviously, because I've always been blessed in the looks department. I've just got lucky, bein' so handsome. As I've got older, it's just got better and better. I've kept me lustrous, full 'ead of 'air and got even more muscular. I'm also a great dancer and, as I think the record will show, quite the hit with t'ladies. As for you, I can't pretend to ya that looks aren't important. They are. I can only suggest you dump all t'mirrors in yer 'ouse and try to avoid looking in shop winders.

Prezza

DEAR PREZZA,

I'm 17 and worried I might be gay. I have no sexual feelings for women, but I have a huge crush on this hunky guy at work. I'm terrified of telling my parents – they're very religious and would be devastated. Could I be gay – or should I see how my feelings evolve as I get older?

Tony Mottram
Ashbourne

PREZZA SAYS:

Listen, chum, if you're not chasing skirt at your age, with all them teenage 'ormones running through ya, you're batting for the other bloody side. Don't get me wrong, now. I don't think there's owt wrong with bein' gay. Some of me best friends have spoken to 'em and say they're allright. We even had a couple of 'em in the Cabinet, an' all. I just didn't like to sit near 'em.

Prezza

DEAR PREZZA,

I've been after my boss's job for more than ten years but he just won't pack it in, even though he's long past his sell-by date. Every now and again, just to get me excited, he hints he'll retire. But he never does. He's just messing me around. Nearly everyone accepts I should be in his job. What should I do? I've even thought about having him bumped off.

G Brown
London

PREZZA SAYS:

Aye, there's nowt more bloody irksome than some jumped-up incompetent little tinpot general clogging up the top of a firm with all the real talent underneath propping him up. Believe me, I've got friends in t'same boat. Tell him straight up how ya feel. If he still won't take the hint, I reckon yer bumpin'-off idea is sound as a pound. I've even gorra couple o' mobile numbers, if you want ter go down that route.

Prezza

DEAR PREZZA,

My husband is lazy, selfish and rude. We've been together 18 years and he never helps with the housework or the kids even though he's out of work. The place is a pig-sty and I'm too embarrassed to have friends round. If I ever dare to tell him how I feel, he tells me to shut up.

Enid Pringle
Bardon-in-the-Beans, Suffolk

PREZZA SAYS:

Oh, that's bloody rich, that is. How do you think HE feels coming home from 'ard day queuing at t'benefit office to find his 'ouse in a state and you bloody whining about it? It's about time you got off yer fat arse and sorted your own bloody life out, woman. No wonder he tells ya to shut up. I couldn't 'ave put it better meself.

Prezza

DEAR PREZZA,

I've been having an affair with a girl who works for me, behind my wife's back. We've been married 40 years and she's been unswervingly loyal. But oddly enough I feel no remorse. It's actually been rather liberating. This girl is much younger than me and such a breath of fresh air. We even had sex in a hotel room when my wife was waiting for me in the lobby downstairs. And sometimes we do it with the door to my office wide open. Why do I not feel an ounce of guilt?

Frank Demarco
Spalding

PREZZA SAYS:

Because you're a despicable bloody 'uman bein', that's why. This woman has stayed with you through thick 'n' thin. Then, the moment temptation comes along, yer after this floozy like a rat oop drainpipe. Hang yer bloody 'ead in shame. You wouldn't catch me doin' summat like that.

Prezza

DEAR PREZZA,

I'm terrified I'm going to fail my exams. I was very close to my mum but she died three months ago and I haven't been able to concentrate since. The grief is just too much. But these exams are crucial if I'm to become a lawyer, which is what I know my mum would have wanted. I'm so depressed, and have had to be prescribed Prozac. Is there anything I can do?

Fiona Proby
Haywards Heath

PREZZA SAYS:

You can bloody well cheer up, lass, for starters. Worse things happen at sea… and I should know, I worked on a cruise ship. Listen, depression is all in t'mind. I think it were that famous comedian Monty Python what said, 'Always look on t'bright side o' life…' – and that's my motto. For what it's worth, I failed me 11-plus. That wasn't due to grief, mind. It were due to stupidity.

Prezza

DEAR PREZZA,

I'm worried what a shallow person I've become. I surf the Internet constantly looking for girls on dating sites. Then I meet them, have sex with them and dump them as fast as I can. I've gone through dozens in the last six months. My mum says it's because a girl I really cared about when I was a student cheated on me – and I now treat all women with contempt. I don't want to be like this. I'm 23 now and I want a long, fulfilling, happy relationship just like everyone else.

> Damian Bladderworth
> Cheddington Gorge, Somerset

PREZZA SAYS:

What the bloody 'eck for, ya daft ha'p'orth? Yer must be out of yer mind, lad. Listen, that Internet's a bloody marvel for pulling birds – and pulling birds is what you should do when yer 23. Plenty o' time later for saddling yerself with one for good. Remember me motto, son: 'When you're on yer death bed, it's the shags you DID have that you'll remember, not t'ones you didn't have.'

> **Prezza**

DEAR PREZZA,

I'm caught in the middle of two feuding colleagues at work and it's really getting me down. It seems like an hour doesn't pass by without one of them walking into my office to moan about the other and ask me to speak to them. I'm fed up playing piggy in the middle. It's lucky I don't have much work on at the moment, or I'd get nothing done.

Gervaise Hardcastle
Lyme Regis

PREZZA SAYS:

Aye, mate, we've all been there. I can't name names, like, for security reasons, but these two numbskulls at me work are always carpin' on about each other. They're like a pair o' bloody kids. One can't stand sight of t'other – and, worse still, they live right near each other. I'm forever 'aving to sort t'buggers out. Now then, ya say y'aven't much work on at t'moment, which may be the kind of job I'm after when I'm sacked as DPM. Where do you work, exactly?

Prezza

DEAR PREZZA,

My husband used to be quite a catch – young-at-heart, an athlete in the bedroom, a career full of potential and a twinkly grin that would melt your heart. He's now become a two-faced, odious ball of blubber who has – and I shudder at the thought – recently been caught dipping his nib in a female colleague's ink well, and his career is fast disappearing down the toilet. What should I do?

Name withheld
London area

PREZZA SAYS:

Flippin' 'eck, Pauline, I told you not to contact me at work.

Prezza

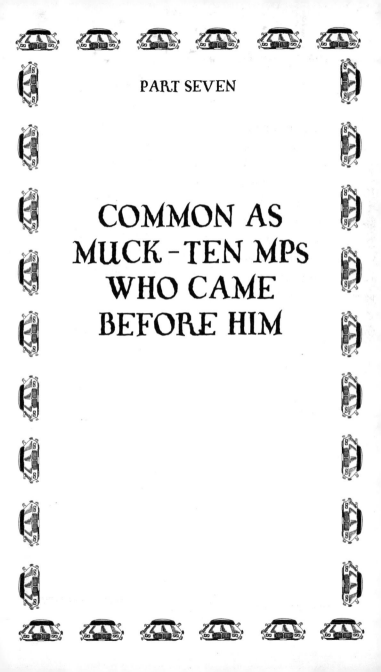

PART SEVEN

COMMON AS
MUCK-TEN MPs
WHO CAME
BEFORE HIM

John Prescott wasn't the first, and won't be the last. Here are the Commons shaggers of modern times whose shame-faced ranks he has joined.

JOHN PROFUMO

The most famous Commons sex scandal of them all involved the married Tory War Secretary who had a fling with showgirl Christine Keeler in 1963 at the same time she was bedding a Russian naval attaché. Profumo denied it in the Commons, but Keeler went public and his career was over.

CECIL PARKINSON

The Tory Trade Secretary quit in 1983 after admitting an affair with his secretary Sara Keays, during which he fathered a daughter, Flora. After four years in the political wilderness, he re-emerged in Maggie Thatcher's Cabinet in 1987.

JEFFREY ARCHER

The one-time Tory MP and Deputy Party Chairman ended up doing time over a liaison with a prostitute in 1987. He won £500,000 libel damages from the *Daily Star* over the allegation but years later was convicted of perjury during the trial and jailed for four years.

RON BROWN

A hot-headed Scottish Labour MP, famous for hurling the Commons mace to the floor during an ill-tempered Poll Tax debate, was fined £1,000 in 1990 for wrecking the flat of an ex-lover with whom he was reputed to have frolicked in a Commons shower. He was cleared of stealing her knickers though.

PADDY ASHDOWN

The Lib Dem leader admitted an affair with a secretary, earning him the nickname Paddy Pantsdown (the *Sun*, 1992). But the fact he came clean over the fling saved his political skin and he remained leader for another seven years.

DAVID MELLOR

Married with two kids at the time, the Tory Heritage Secretary quit in 1992 after an affair with actress Antonia de Sancha. He was said to have bedded her while wearing the strip of his beloved Chelsea, a story which sadly turned out to be untrue.

JOHN MAJOR AND EDWINA CURRIE

The most incredible Commons coupling of all. Edwina made the four-year fling public in 2002, 15 years after it ended and after both she and Major had left office. At the time of the affair, both were married with young kids. The image of the dull-as-ditchwater, pea-loving future PM and the Thatcherite bossyboots getting it on stunned the nation.

RON DAVIES

Labour high-flier whose sexual adventures brought about a spectacular downfall. Tony Blair's Welsh Secretary got the boot after being caught seeking gay sex on Clapham Common. He washed up on the Welsh Assembly, only to be caught in 2003 at a notorious gay haunt – where he claimed to be looking for 'badgers'. Davies later quit the Labour Party.

BORIS JOHNSON

The Tory MP for Henley was sacked as shadow Arts Minister in 2004 over an extra-marital affair with magazine columnist Petronella Wyatt, which he initially denied. He has recently been brought back to David Cameron's front bench.

MARK OATEN

He briefly challenged for the leadership of the Lib Dems in 2006 while knowing a giant skeleton in his cupboard was waiting to come out. The married father of two was exposed for a dalliance with a rent boy and quit frontline politics. Amazingly, he blamed a mid-life crisis brought about by hair loss.

PART EIGHT

GRUBBY'S UP – PRESCOTT'S RECIPE FOR LOVE

BREAKFAST IN BED

An oft-overlooked opportunity for romance, a shared breakfast can refresh and rejuvenate a couple after an evening of lovemaking, re-energising them for more physical adventure in the morning. In order to give yourself and your lover that morning boost, Prezza recommends any, or all, of the following.

There's nothing like the remains of last night's takeaway to recapture the mood and set you up for some lazy Sunday sex. Bring your partner a cold plate of chow mein or even a reheated curry and drive them prawn crackers in the bedroom.

John doesn't recommend attempting a Full English breakfast in bed, as 'you never know when a sausage'll roll off your plate into an awkward hole'. Better off giving your love something to grab hold of – the classic fried egg, chips and bacon sandwich is guaranteed to add some sauce to any cosy breakfast – brown sauce that is.

Show her some truly smooth behaviour with a healthy smoothie shake. Take a bar of chocolate, some cream, a pint of milk and a handful of sugar and whisk up a pint of health that'll whisk her off her feet. Really, she won't be able to get up for hours after all that lot. Perfect for the act of love.

'Blood-red eyes at night, Prezza's delight; Champers in the morning, stops Prezza yawning.' Nothing beats a little tipple to kickstart the day. Indulge in a couple of bottles of the good stuff to ensure all pistons are firing. Well, perhaps all pistons but one.

LUNCH

Whether you're out with the wife, or masticating with the mistress, a lovers' luncheon is something to relish. Taken early, that midday meal for two can be the perfect chance to re-fuel and relax after a romp-filled morning. Or dine a little later as a prelude to some afternoon loving. Prezza, the Carnivore Casanova extraordinaire, is a seasoned pro in timing a lunch to both end one sex session and to prepare for the next – on the same day, of course. Speaking of courses, here's a few tips from a man who knows how to give a tip…

The 'light lunch' is, as a concept, offensive to any gastronome and, in practice, barely enough for a gnome. Any man worth his weight in fat should aim for at least three courses over which to woo the women. Go for traditional fayre – game, foie gras, pies and roast potatoes, and rich desserts swimming in custard. To ensure that your indigestion leads to mutually agreed sexual indiscretions, make sure you get some under-the-table fumbling in for starters. Literally for starters – you want the sexual energy to be in full force by main course.

It goes without saying that alcohol is essential kit for any love match. Forget wine by the glass, only a bottle will open the love throttle and you'll need a bottle per course. Remember the Prescott mantra: *If she orders water, you shouldn't 'ave brought her, but Sauvignon Blanc equals a bonk.*

DINNER

The daddy of dining experiences, the master of meals. A romantic dinner in a steak restaurant will set both the lady and the gentleman up for an evening of primal passion. Though, as Prezza observes, if she asks for T-Bone she's no lady, and you're probably in for a 'rare' treat.